Color, Cut & Fold

T0044734

OCEAN ANIMALS

PRACTICE SCISSOR SKILLS!

Let's get started!

All you need is a pair of scissors, a glue stick, and markers, colored pencils, or crayons! There are stickers to add to your creations when you have finished.

1

Carefully pull out the page you want along the perforation.

2

Color both sides of the page with markers, pencils, or crayons.

3

Start at the dot.

Starting at the dot, cut out the picture around the dashed line.

Cut around dashed lines.

Fold along dotted lines.

Where to cut?

Cut along dashed lines like this.

Where to fold?

Fold along dotted lines like this.

Where to glue?

Some of the animals should be folded and glued. Follow the instructions on each page.

Shark

There are more than 400 types of sharks! Their babies are called pups.

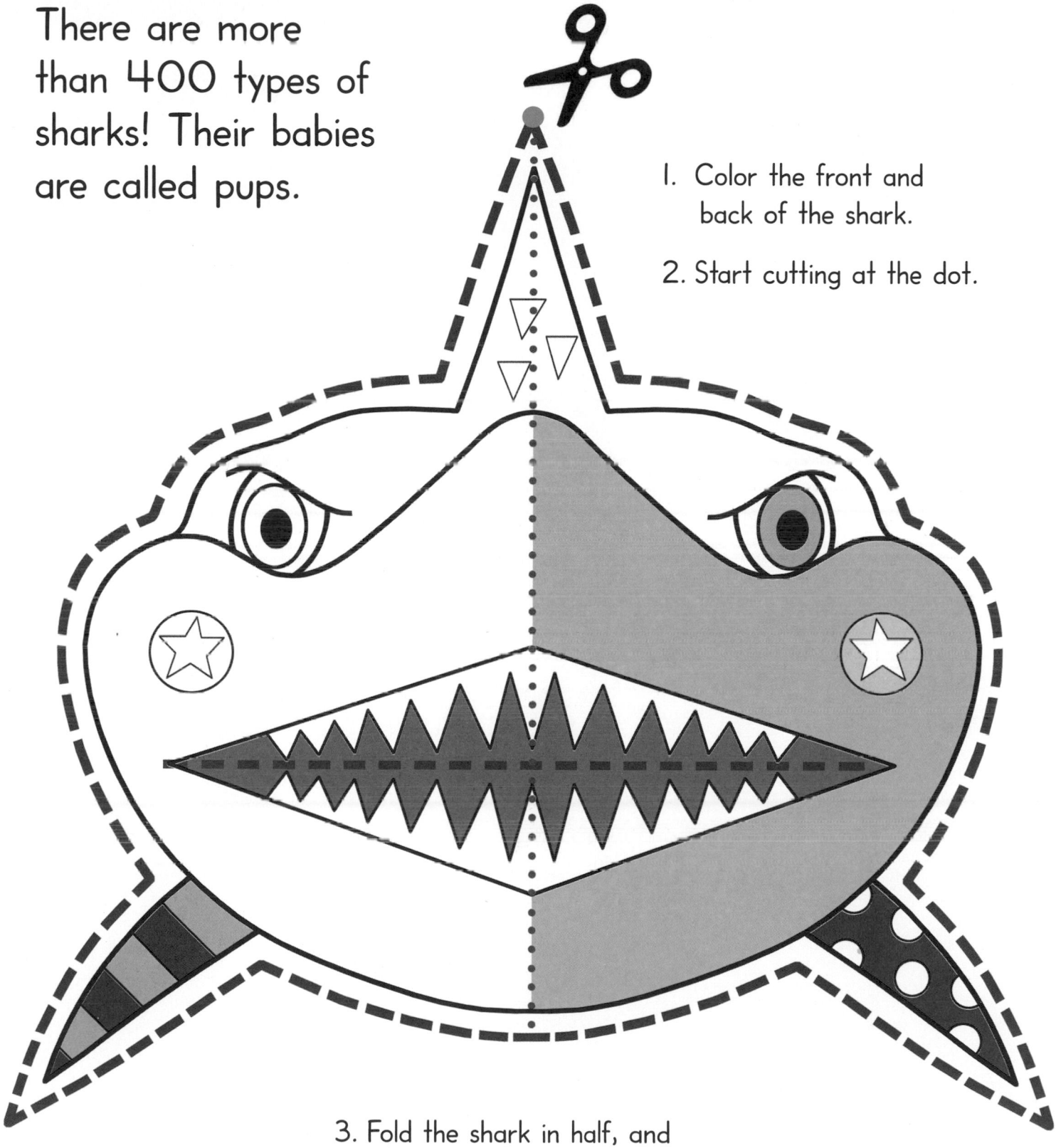

1. Color the front and back of the shark.
2. Start cutting at the dot.
3. Fold the shark in half, and then cut along the dashed line at the center of the mouth.

4. Unfold, and then find stickers to decorate your shark.

Dolphin

1. Color the front and back of the dolphin.
2. Start cutting at the dot.

Dolphins are very smart, and they love to play.

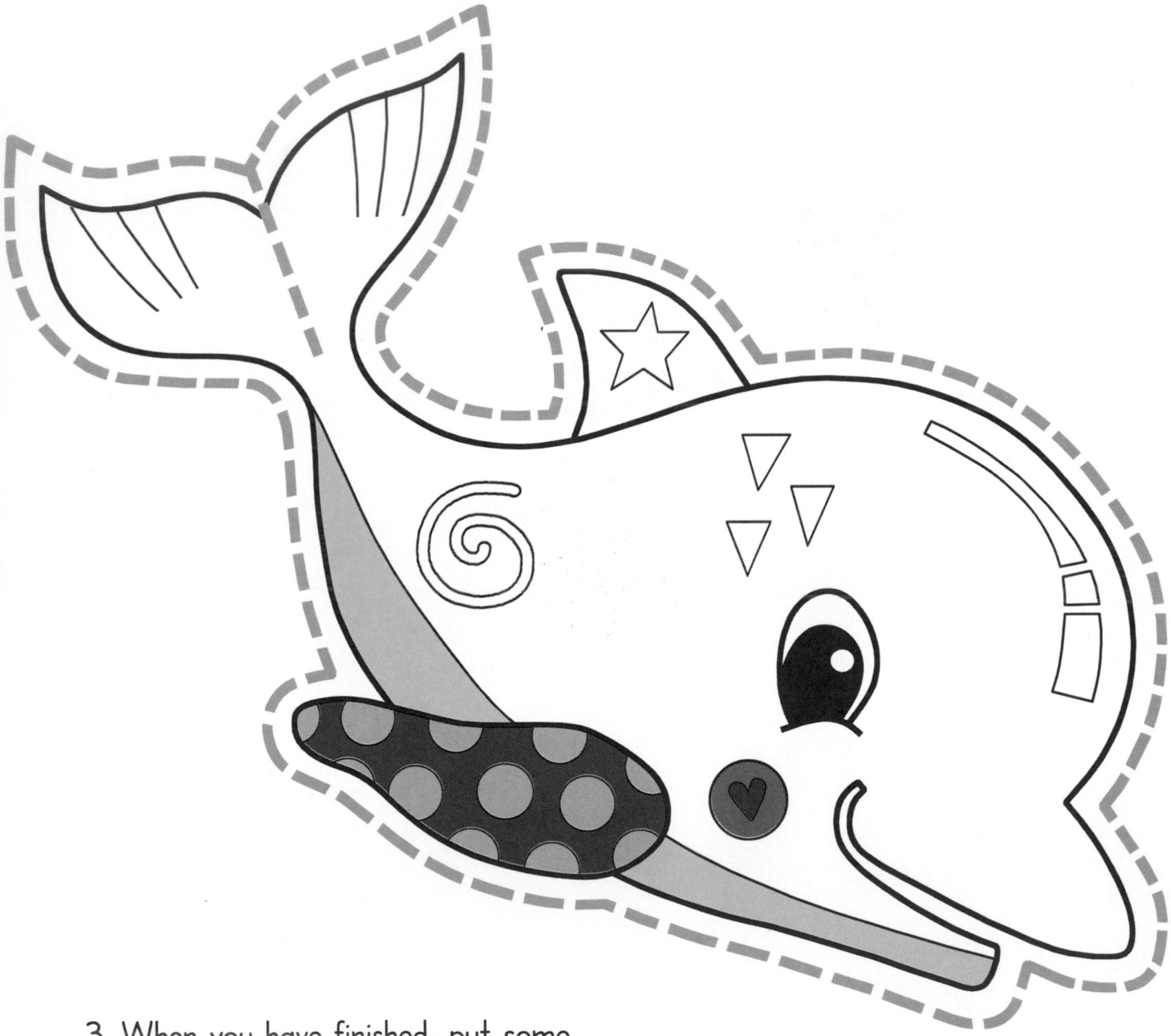

3. When you have finished, put some stickers on your dolphin!

Sea Turtle

Sea turtles can live for over 100 years!

1. Color the front and back of the sea turtle.
2. Start cutting at the dot.

3. Fold all of the dotted lines toward the back of the turtle.

4. Glue each tab marked "Glue" under the next flap to make your sea turtle stand up.

Jellyfish

Some jellyfish glow in the dark.

1. Color the front and back of the jellyfish.
2. Start cutting at the dot.

3. Fold the tentacles along the lines like an accordion.

4. If you want, you can attach a piece of thread to the head and hang your jellyfish.

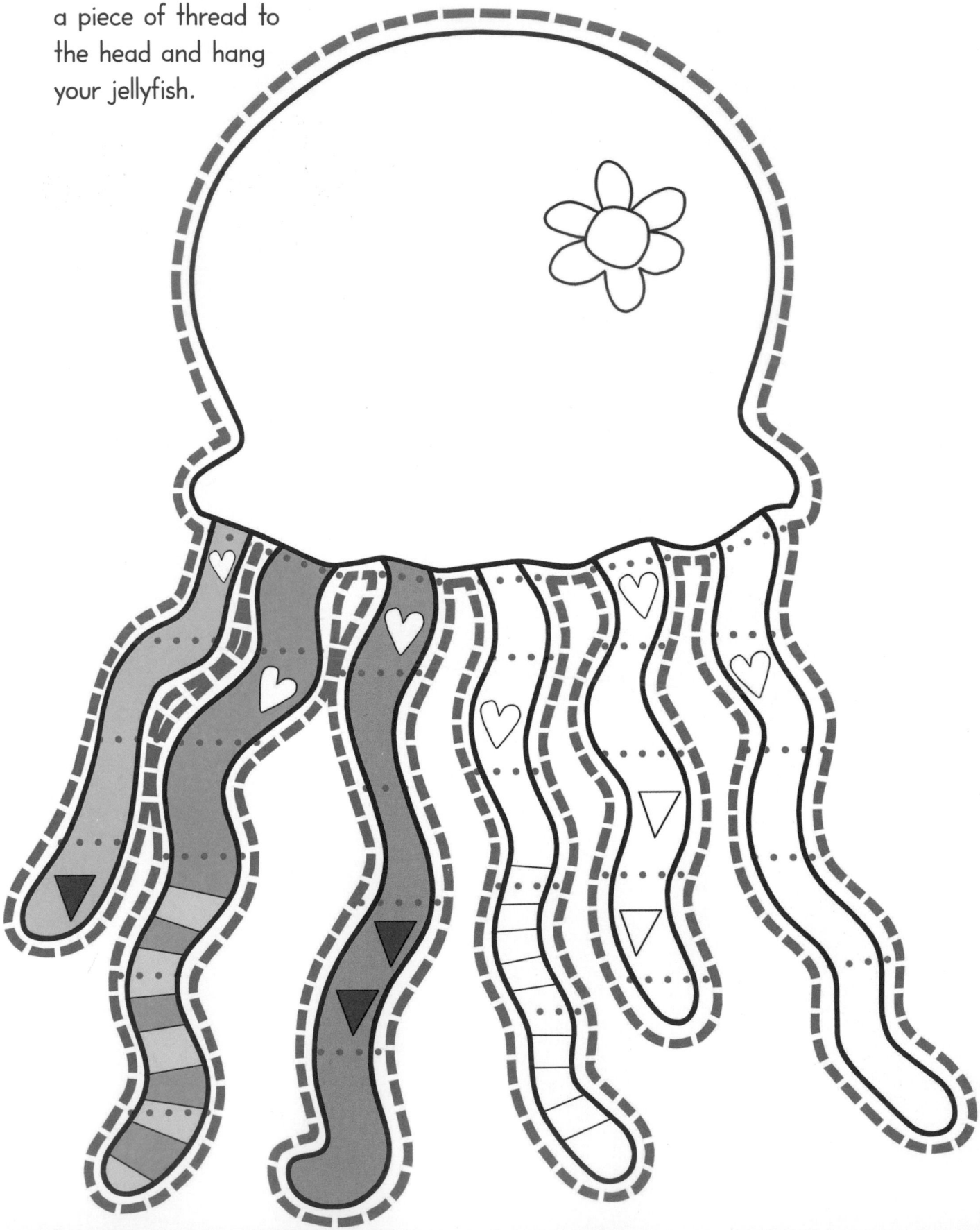

Hermit Crab

Hermit crabs like to decorate their seashell homes with things they find in the ocean.

1. Color the front and back of the hermit crab.
2. Start cutting at the dot.

3. Stick the triangular area under the flap with glue.

4. When you have finished, fold the shell to make the horns stand up.

Ask a grown-up to cut around the head and horns!

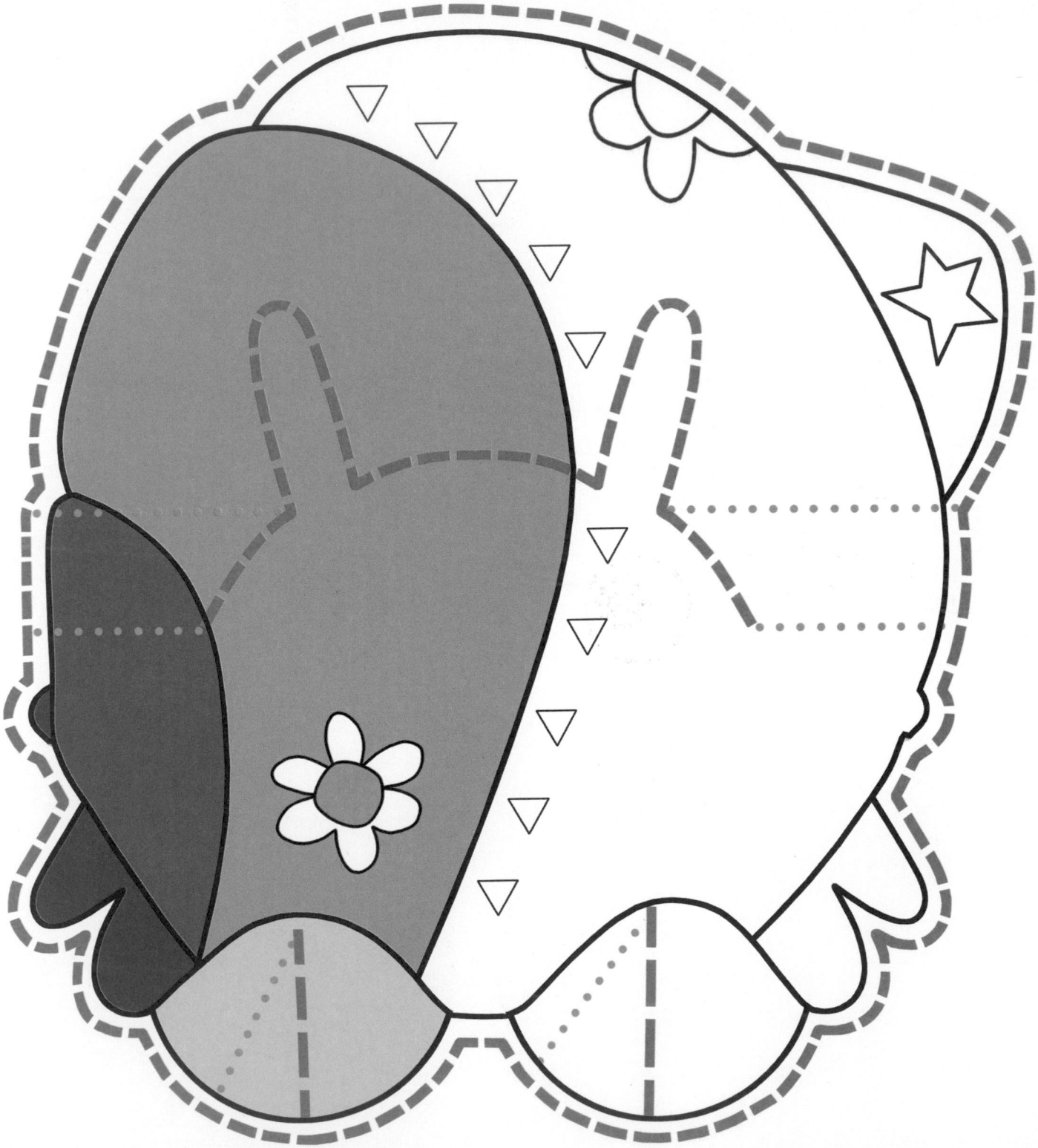

Starfish

Starfish aren't really fish. They are related to sea urchins.

1. Color the front and back of the starfish.
2. Start cutting at the dot.

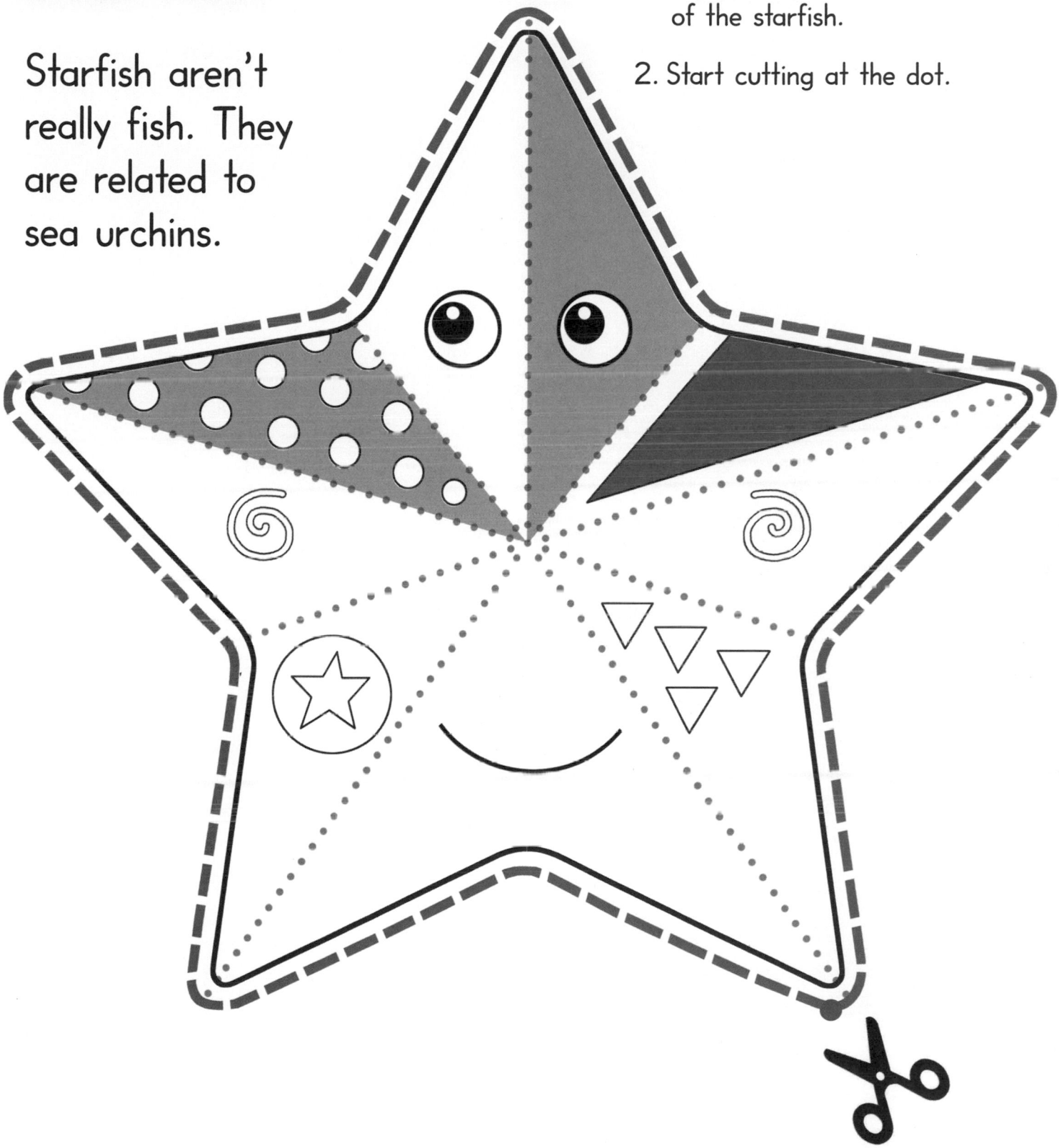

3. When you have finished, fold along the dotted lines to make your starfish stand up.

Angelfish

Marine angelfish often live in coral reefs.

1. Color the front and back of the angelfish.
2. Start cutting at the dot.

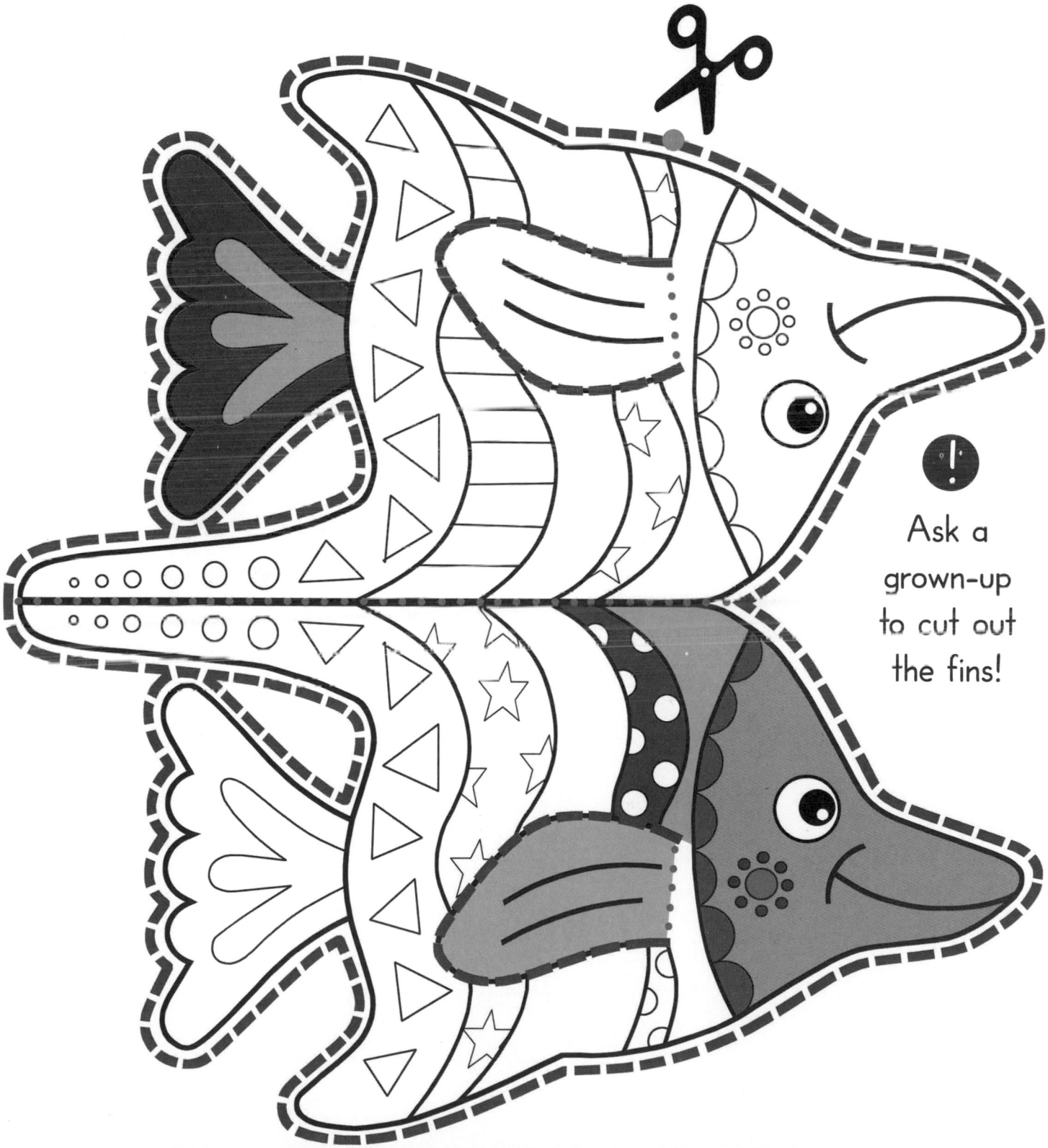

3. Fold the angelfish in half, and fold out the side fins a little.

Lobster

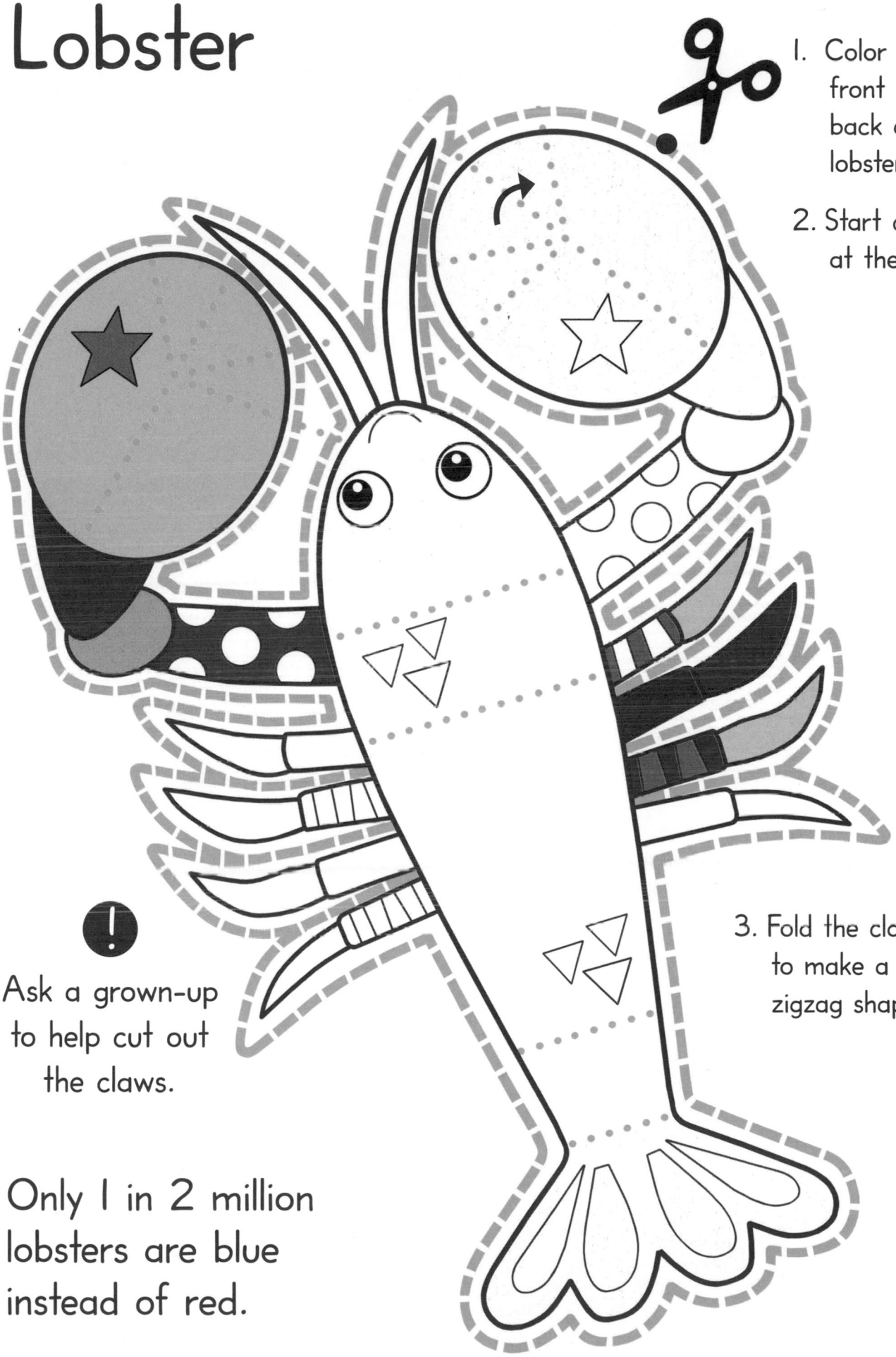

1. Color the front and back of the lobster.
2. Start cutting at the dot.
3. Fold the claws to make a zigzag shape.

Ask a grown-up to help cut out the claws.

Only 1 in 2 million lobsters are blue instead of red.

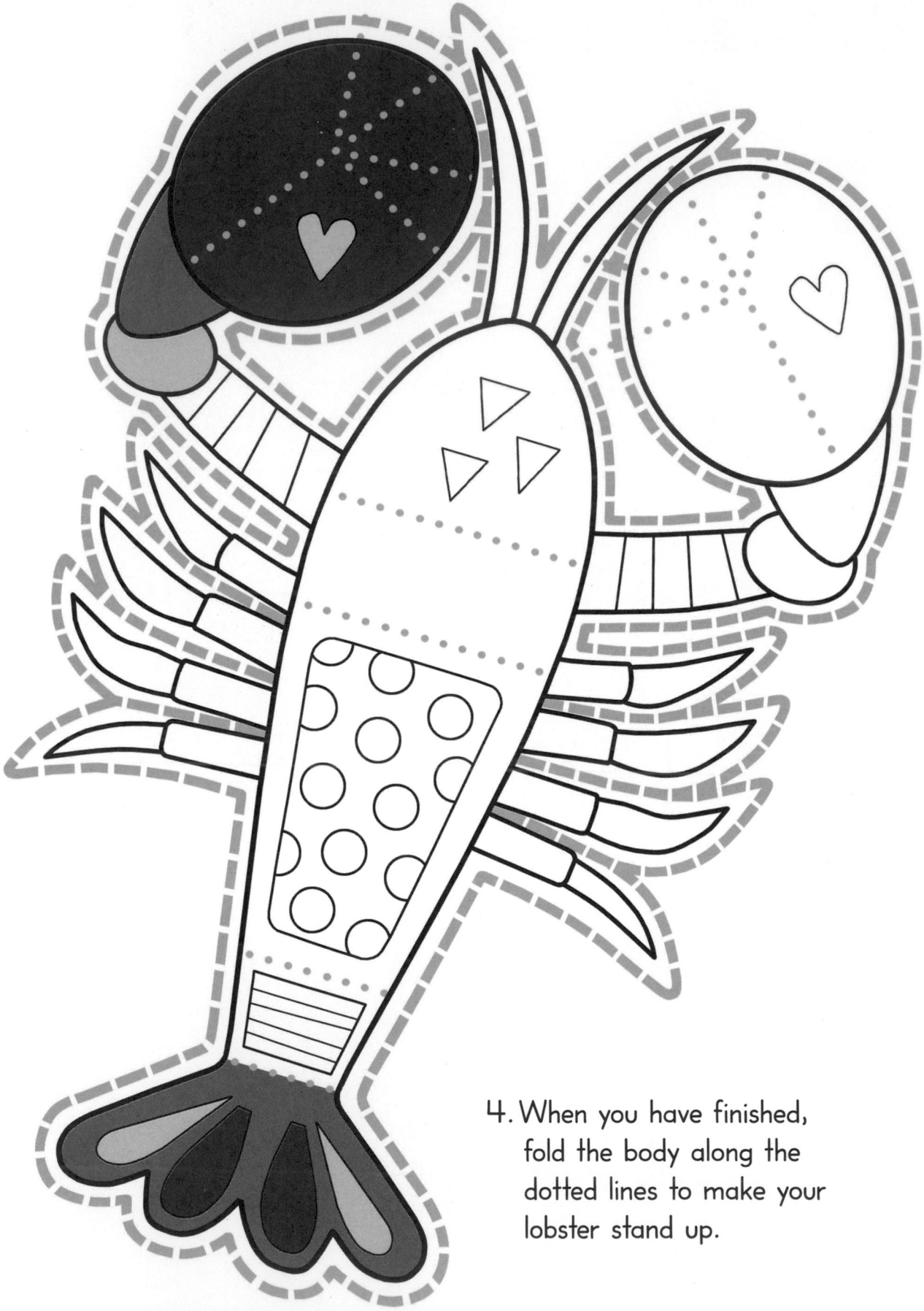

4. When you have finished, fold the body along the dotted lines to make your lobster stand up.

Seashell

Animals called mollusks live in seashells.

1. Color the front and back of the seashell.
2. Start cutting at the dot.

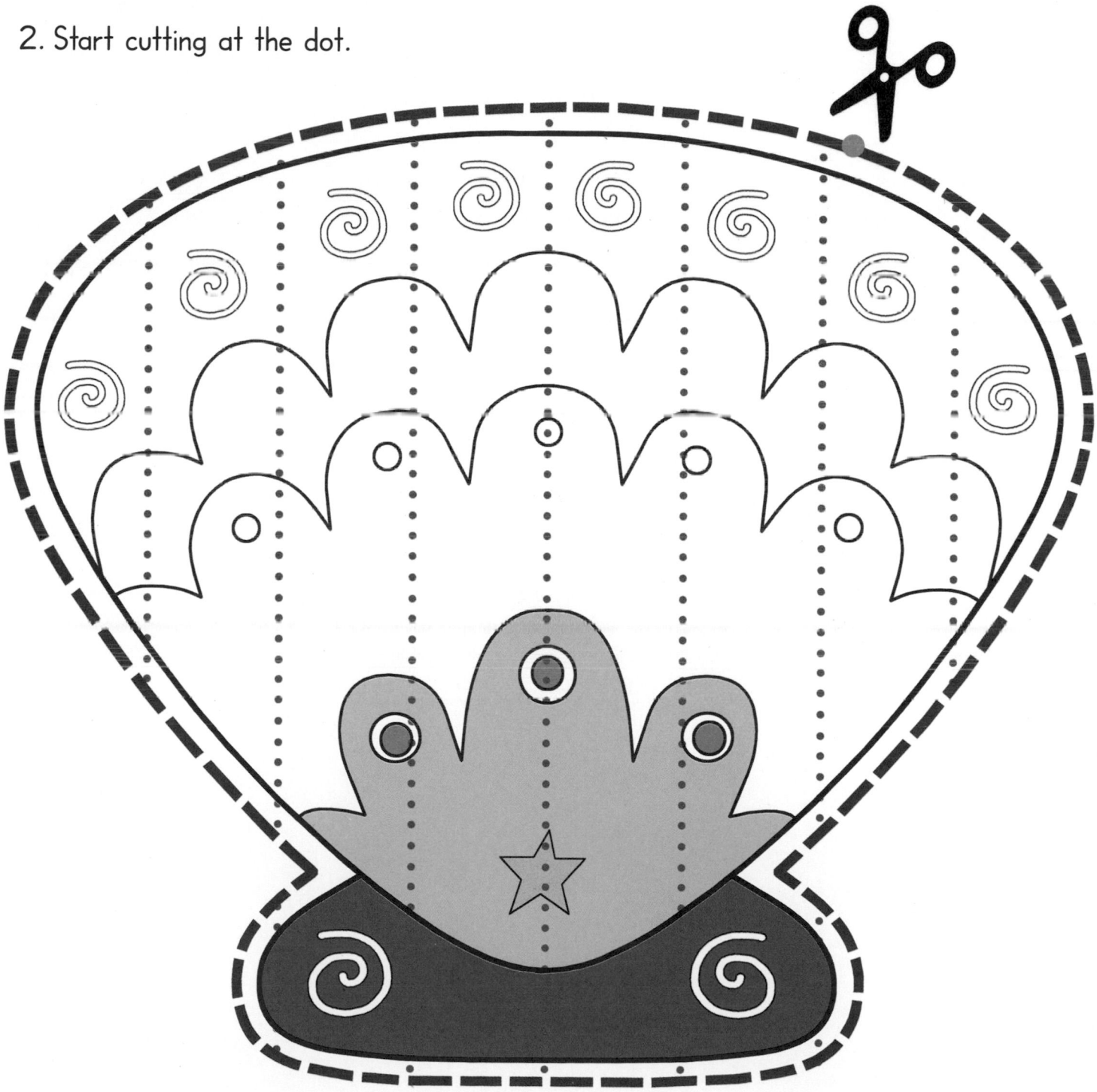

3. Fold along the dotted lines like an accordion. Unfold to make your seashell stand up.

Seahorse

1. Color the front and back of the seahorse.
2. Start cutting at the dot.

Seahorses like to swim in pairs with their friends.

3. Stick the triangle under the flap with glue.

4. If you want, you can attach a piece of thread to the head and hang your seahorse.

Octopus

An octopus has three hearts and eight legs.

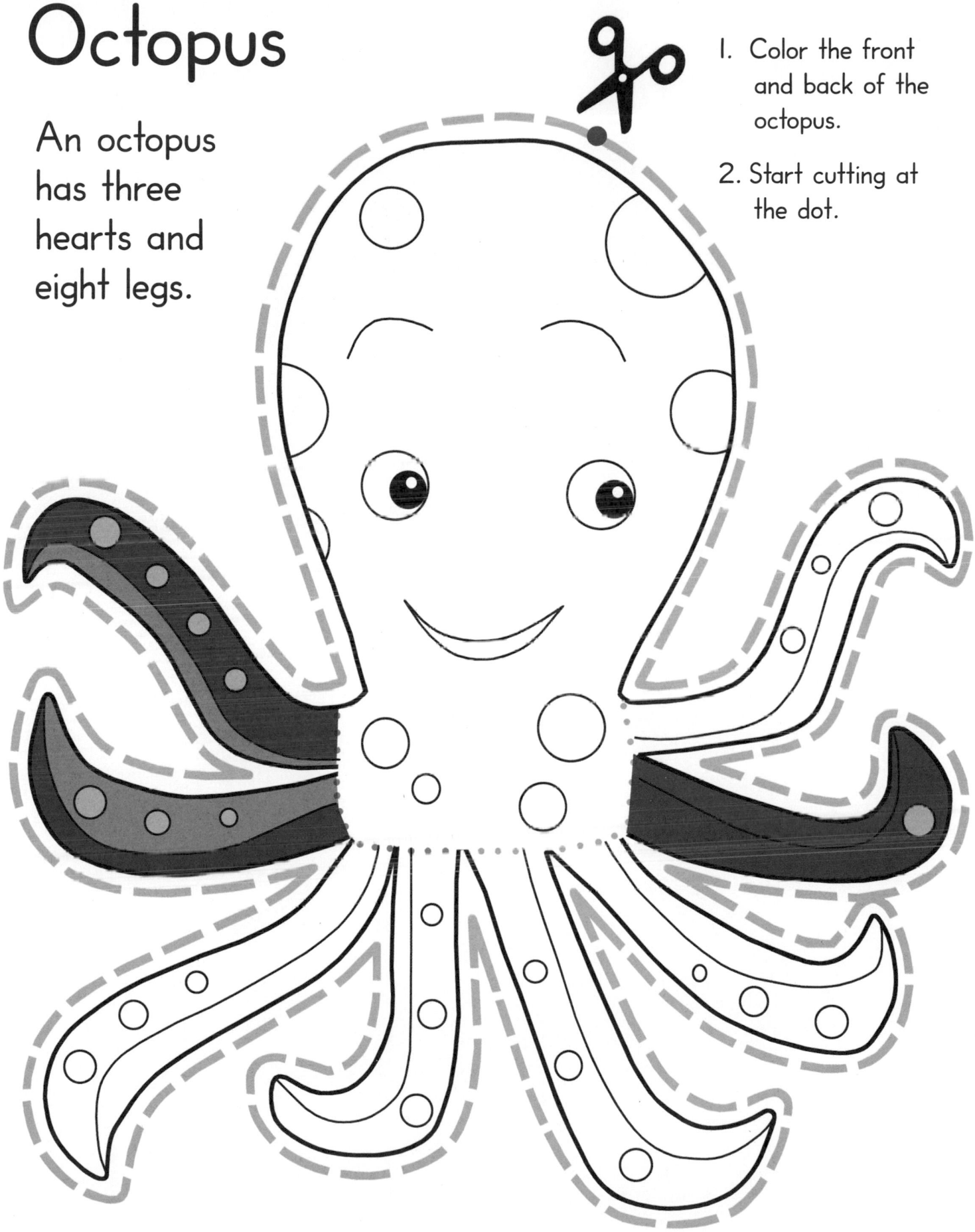

1. Color the front and back of the octopus.
2. Start cutting at the dot.

3. When you have finished, fold the legs a little, and tape your octopus to a window.

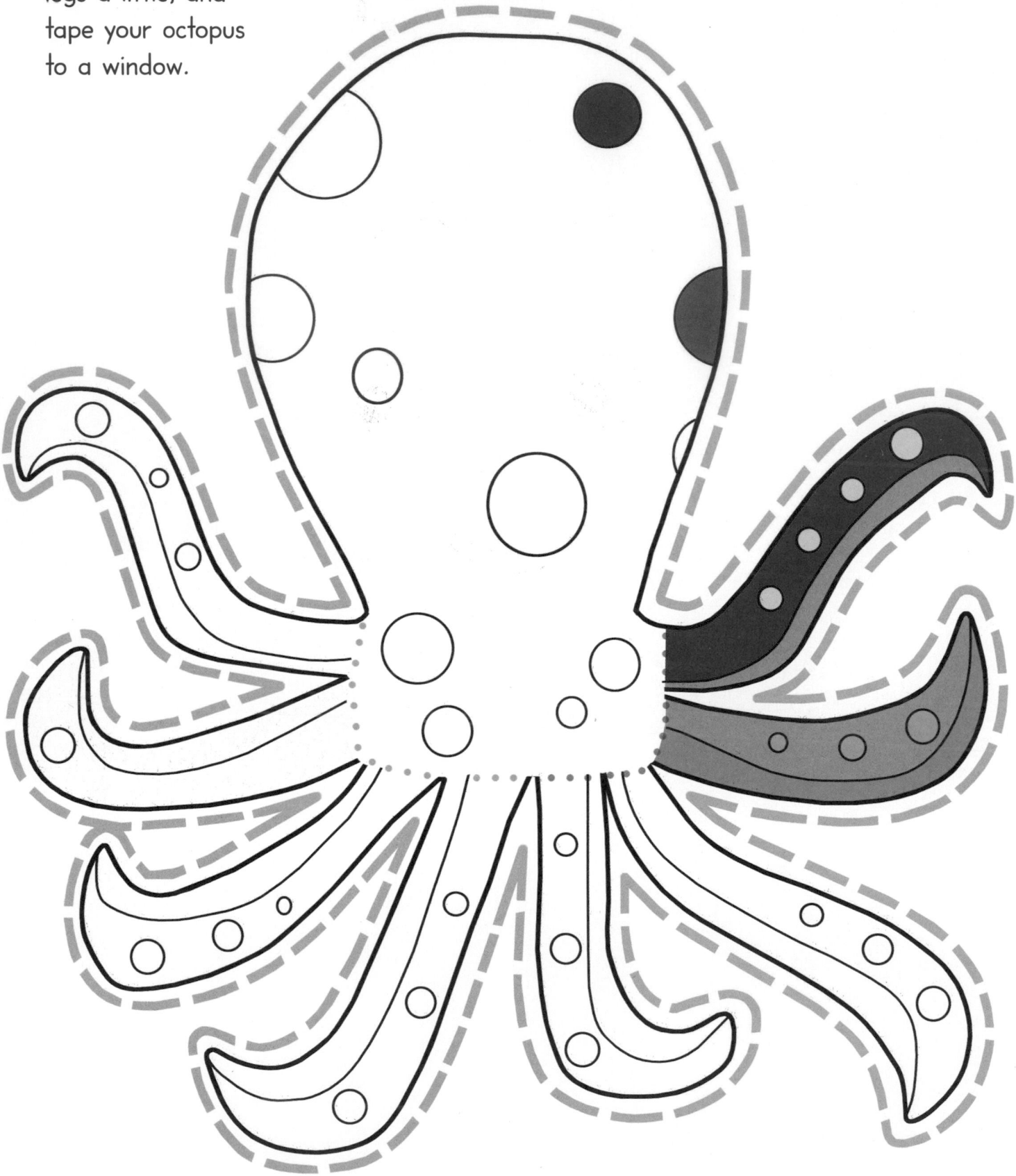

Fish

Fish have gills that let them breathe underwater.

4. When you have finished, add some stickers!

Parrotfish

Parrotfish clean coral by nibbling at its surface.

1. Color the front and back of the parrotfish.
2. Start cutting at the dot.

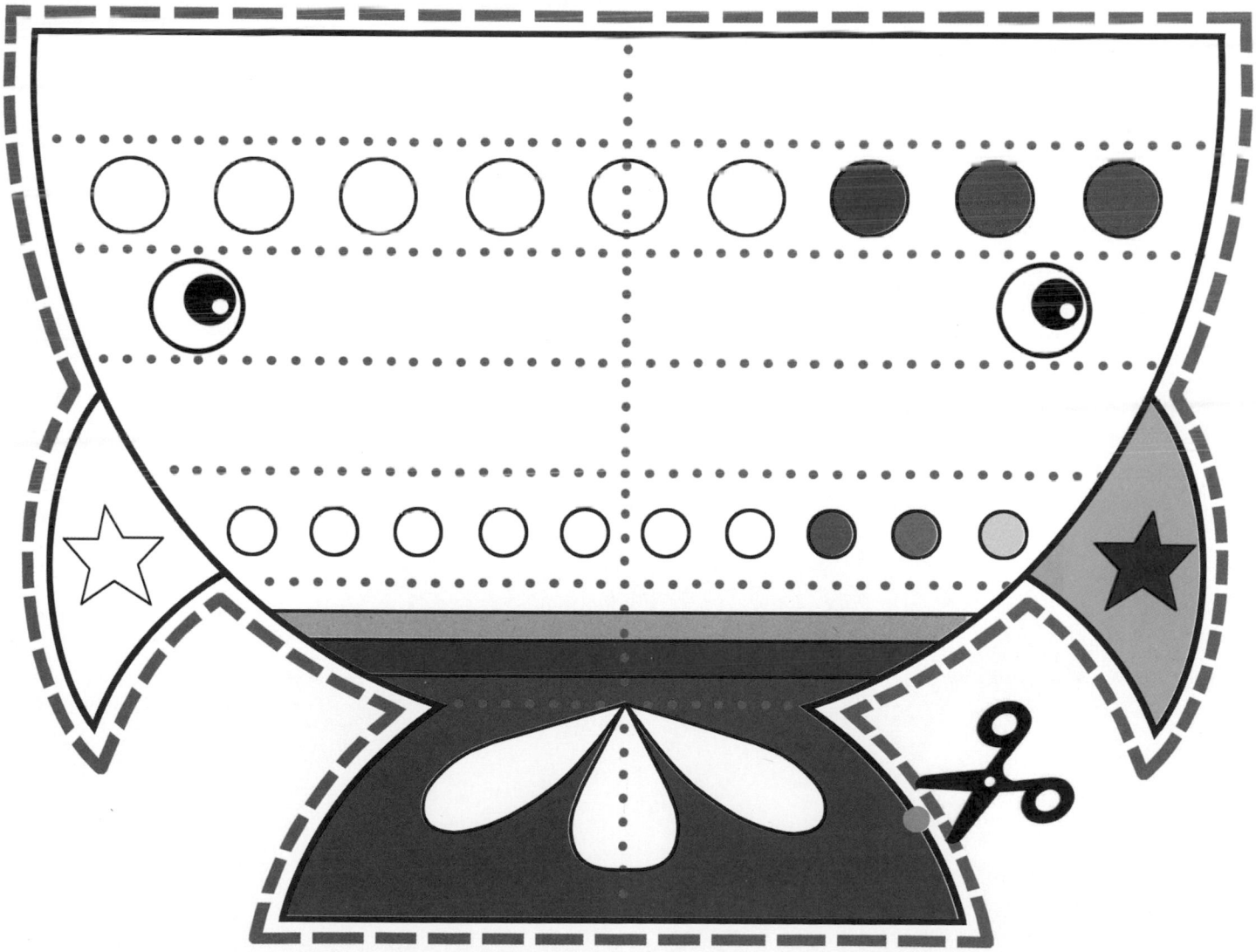

3. Fold the horizontal lines first, like an accordion.

4. Unfold a little, and then fold in half along the center dotted line.

5. Glue the inside together along the blue bar.

Penguin

Penguins can't fly, but they can swim really well.

1. Color the front and back of the penguin.

2. Start cutting at the dot.

3. Fold in half, and then cut the beak.

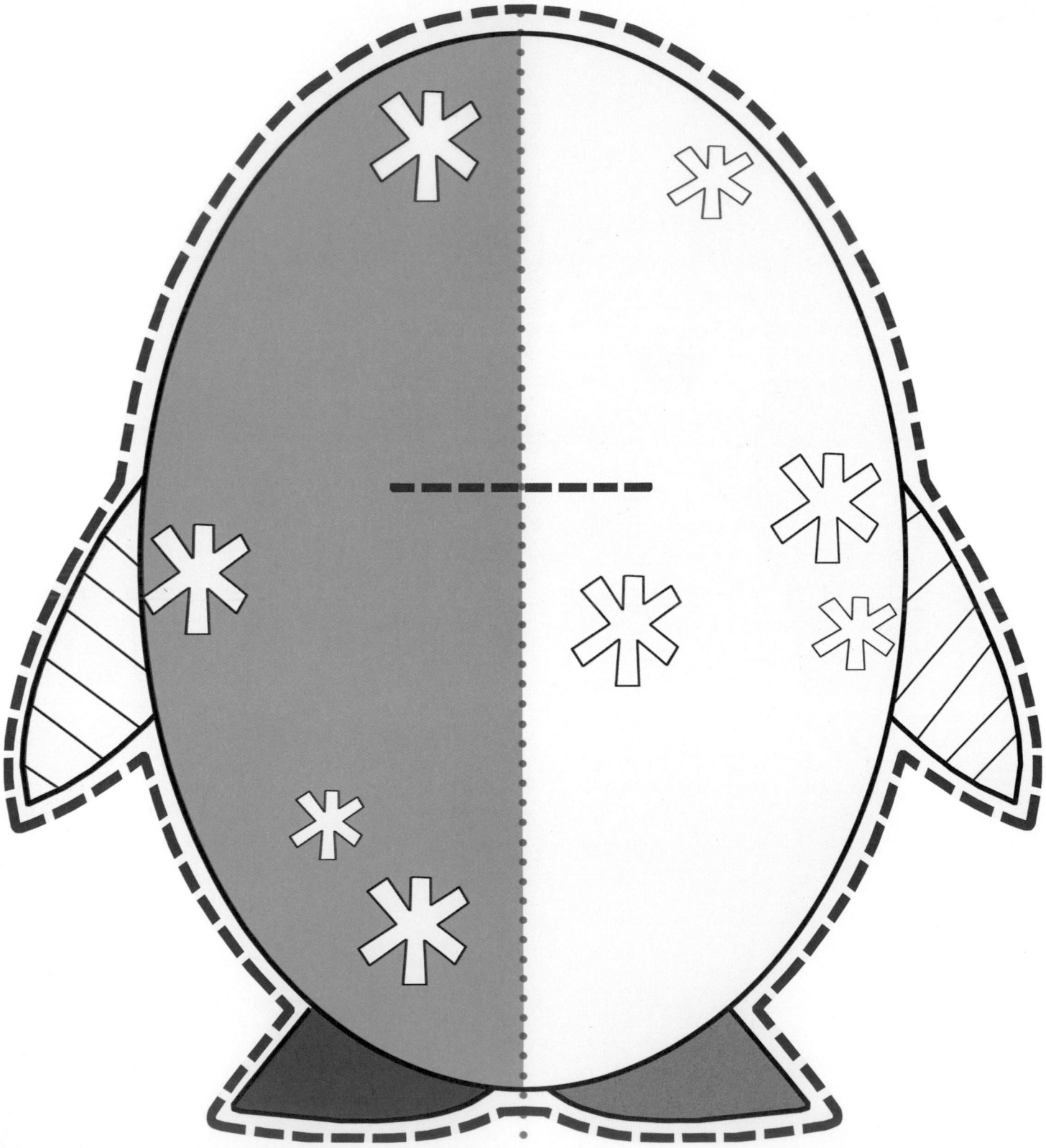

Whale

The blue whale is the largest animal in the world.

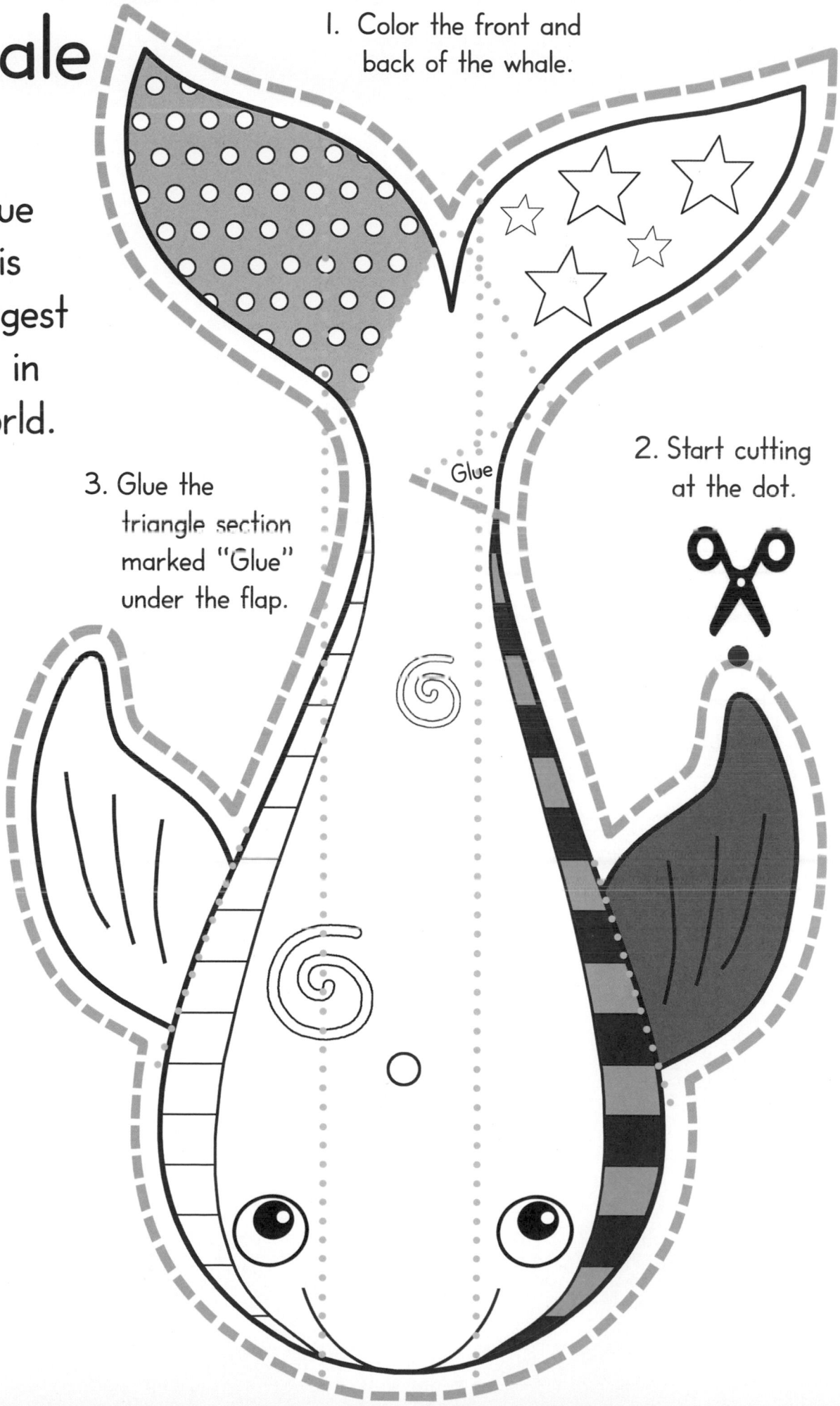

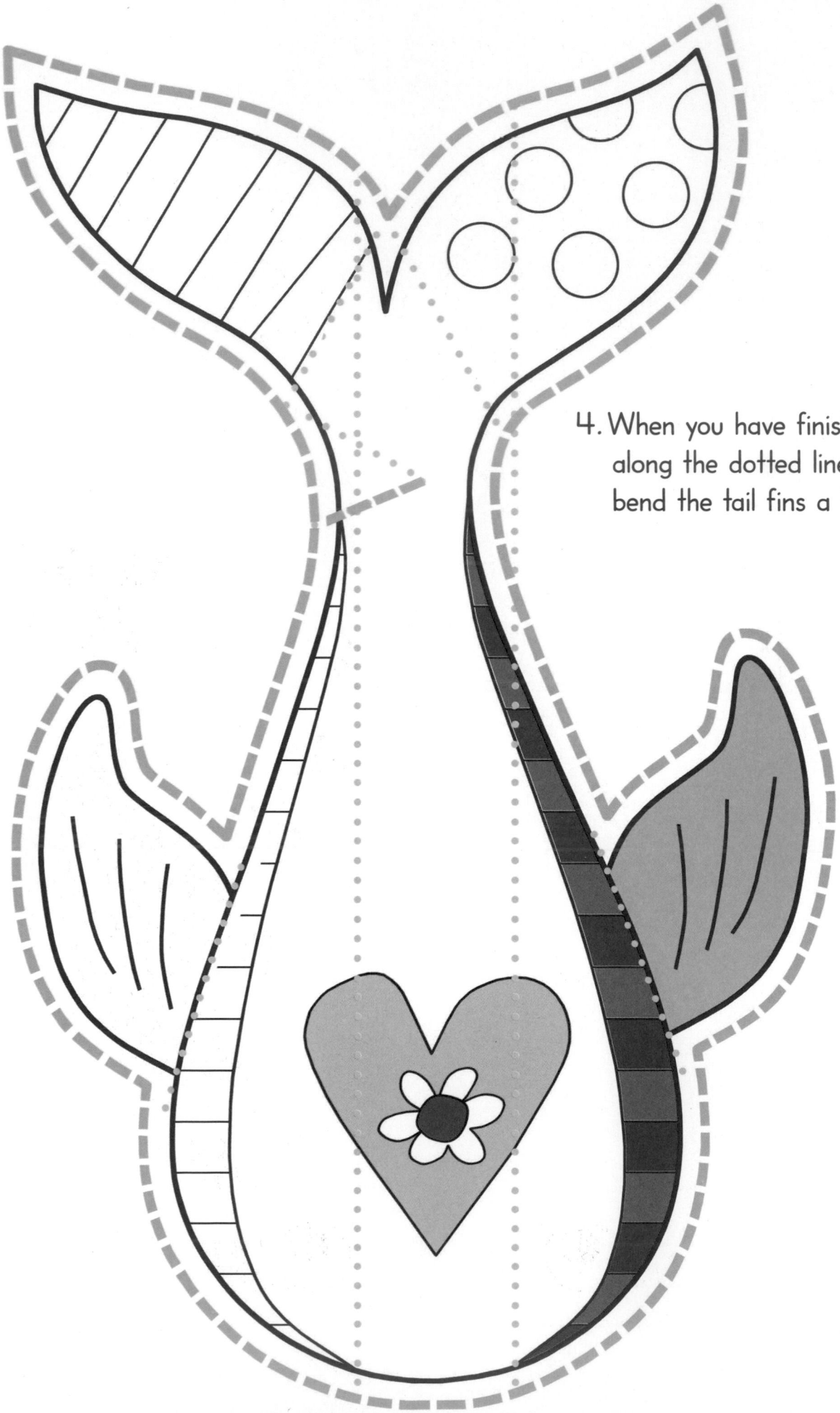

4. When you have finished, fold along the dotted lines, and bend the tail fins a little.